DEATH'S DOOR DENIED

so that the door to life could be opened.

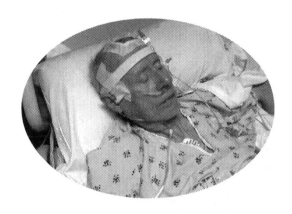

THE MAN THAT SHOULD HAVE DIED,
WOULD HAVE DIED, BUT COULD NOT DIE.

Fred F. Everhart, DVM, JD

authorHOUSE®

AuthorHouse™
1663 Liberty Drive
Bloomington, IN 47403
www.authorhouse.com
Phone: 1-800-839-8640

First published by AuthorHouse 3/10/2011

ISBN: 978-1-4567-3666-8 (e)
ISBN: 978-1-4567-3664-4 (sc)

Library of Congress Control Number: 2011901714

Printed in the United States of America

Any people depicted in stock imagery provided by Thinkstock are models, and such images are being used for illustrative purposes only. Certain stock imagery © Thinkstock.

This book is printed on acid-free paper.

TABLE OF CONTENTS

A PIVOTAL DAY IN MY MEMORY BANK

May in 2009 was the month and year of what would have been, could have been, and should have been my death at eighty-three years of age.

On May 19, 2009, at the Athletic Club in Columbia, Maryland, I was engaged in a short workout with a few pull-ups, then proceeding with a few more exercises. Not long after the pull-ups, I developed a slight headache. This was quite unusual for me, since I had never experienced a headache from the time I had stopped eating red meat twenty-six years before, following a serious heart attack. The headache alerted me to stop the exercise program and head for home.

After arriving at home, I notified my wife, Elaine, that we had better go to the emergency room at the Howard County General Hospital, as I was sure that I was in the process of having a hemorrhagic stroke. This insight from medical knowledge was gained while practicing veterinary medicine and from the fact that I was currently taking the anticoagulant Plavix.

Shortly afterwards, I remember arriving at the hospital and entering the emergency room as Elaine approached the admissions desk. Surprisingly, there was no one in the waiting room. There would be no waiting. That very unusual entrance and fortuitous event foretold the creation of subsequent unanticipated and unforeseeable results. It is the last thing I remember until waking up at Johns Hopkins Bayview Medical Center three days later. According to Elaine, the physician on duty at Howard County General Hospital immediately recognized the seriousness of the event and ordered a CT scan. During this process, I apparently became very ill, with a lot of vomiting. And there was Elaine standing by me, watching me trying to die. Elaine became physically ill herself. She had been told that the prognosis was grave, as I was having a massive brain bleed, an intracerebral hemorrhage that eventually filled up the ventricles of my brain. Her good friend, Barb, was there to support her. Barb would tell me later that when she saw me, she was looking at the image of death. It was then that Elaine told Barb, "I don't think he's going to make it."

THE MEDICAL RECORD
CT SCAN REPORT

The following is an exact copy of the initial medical report:

At the request of: MICHELLE A HENGGELER M.D.

Procedure: HDWO CT HEAD W/O CONTRAST
Name: EVERHART, FRED Phys: Henggeler, Michelle A.
M.D. DOB: 03/25/1926 Age: 83 Sex: M Acct: V00013088059
Loc: ER Exam Date: 05/19/2009 Status: DEP ER Unit No:
M00057979

*EXAM# TYPE/EXAM 001301550 CT/CT HEAD W/O
CONTRAST*
HOWARD COUNTY GENERAL HOSPITAL, INC.

**Results were discussed with Dr. Michele Henggeler,
05/19/2009 at 2:24 p.m.**

INDICATION: Headache, status post heavy lifting. Evaluate
for intracranial bleed.
IMPRESSION: Large parenchymal hematoma centered
within the right temporal lobe with extension into the
ventricular system. There is approximately 5 mm of right to
left subfalcine herniation with a large clot seen within the
right lateral ventricle.
FINDINGS: *Noncontrast CT scan of the brain was obtained
May 19, 2009. There is a large parenchymal hematoma centered
within the right temporal lobe measuring 5.2 cm AP x 3.7 cm*

3

transverse. This hemorrhage extends into the temporal horn of the right lateral ventricle as well as the right lateral ventricle, third ventricle, left lateral ventricle and fourth ventricles There is a large clot seen within the right lateral ventricle with approximately 5 mm of right to left subfalcine herniation. No fractures are seen.
** REPORT SIGNATURE ON FILE 05/26/2009 **
Reported And Signed By: VICTOR BRACEY M.D.

Later, Elaine would tell me that God must have intervened because she had been told that Johns Hopkins Bayview Medical Center was recognized as one of the leading stroke centers in the country, and that is where the Medevac helicopter took me. I now regret that in my unconscious state, I was unable to enjoy the experience of the helicopter ride.

Elaine had called our children, Greg, Missy, Bunbun, and April, three of the four being from out of state. Dr. Greg Kang, who is a physical medicine physician in Myrtle Beach, received the phone call for his wife, my daughter Missy. He called the neurologist in an effort to get the complete story from a medical point of view. Later, he was to tell me that the information from the CT report revealed that it was a death sentence, based upon his experience. He then told Missy that she had better get up to Maryland right away because he didn't think her father was going to make it. She left immediately from Myrtle Beach, South Carolina, as did my son Gregory from the same city. At about the same time, my daughter Bunbun left from Martinsville, Virginia. My youngest daughter April fortunately didn't have far to travel from Halethorpe, Maryland.

CONFUSION

Three days after arriving at Johns Hopkins Bayview Medical Center, I awakened to discover my arms tied to the side rails of the bed. The neurosurgeon had made an opening in my skull and had inserted a tube to drain the blood from my brain in an effort to relieve the intracranial pressure. The medical staff wanted me to be still and rest, but this was extremely frustrating to me. I needed to move my arms; I felt a need to sit up and get out of the bed. There was a lot of activity in the room when the neurologist arrived to question me.

"Do you know where you are?" he asked.

"Yes, I'm at the Howard County Hospital," was my immediate reply.

"No," he said, "You are in Johns Hopkins Bayview."

"Oh."

"Do you know what the date is?"

I answered, after some thought, "January 1, 1929."

"No", he corrected me, "the date is May 22, 2009."

Again, "Oh." I knew that I needed to remember that date. Later, he asked me the same questions, and I was pleased that my answers were correct. His interrogation was needed to evaluate my mental state and to further determine a prognosis.

Elaine tells me that it was during this time that I asked her, "Who's that man behind you?"

She replied, "There's no man behind me." I made no issue of it, but she believes that the "man" must have been an angel or Jesus. I thought no more about it.

Over the period of the next several days, my legs and back began to be very painful. My calves were beginning to cramp. Until now, I had considered myself to be very blessed because advancing age had never brought on any back or leg discomfort. I had continued to be very agile and would rather run than walk. That made it imperative for me to get out of bed. That, at the very least, could enable me to stand on my legs. I continued to attempt to untie my restraints on my wrists. When I succeeded in doing so and was in the process of getting out of bed, the attendants, with a lot of justifiable scolding, tied mittens on my hands to prevent me from untying my wrists, which were again secured to the bedside railings. My daughters, who were there and knew my stubborn streak, warned the nurse that I would be able to circumvent that measure also.

Some time later, with great determination, I was able to remove the mittens, untie the restraint, and begin crawling over the side rail when I heard the excited voice of the nurse exclaiming, "Papa, Papa, what are you trying to do, kill yourself?" I believe that she was Filipino. The only reason I identify her in this manner is because of my great respect for those of that nationality. Everyone of her nationality with whom I have ever come in contact has been extremely kind and compassionate. After this episode, the staff knew me as "Houdini."

My wife Elaine and her friend Barb had been with me during the whole event of my stroke. My children, two of whom are nurses, were also present during much of the time. Yet, during this period, there was enough confusion on my part that my memory was like a fading mist. Elaine and my children have filled in some of the missing gaps.

My daughter April reminded me later that as a result of my frustrations, I asked her to "Go get Mason to run these people out of the room."

A nurse asked, "Who is Mason?"

April said, "That's his German shepherd dog."

I vaguely remember many of my good friends visiting me, as did three of my grandchildren, Jamie, Luke, and Jordan, from out of state. There could be no better support than their physical presence.

I understand that the pastor from my church, Dr. Mark Meyer, was there every day. I well remember him reading to me the Sermon on the Mount from the Bible. I was greatly surprised at my lack of reaction to those words. One of my favorite stories in the Bible, this was read in an effort to uplift and inspire me. It didn't. It appeared to me at the time to be merely words and nothing more, without the inspiration I had anticipated. I attempted to understand my lack of a more positive reaction. It was beyond me. Everything in me told me that I should have really been uplifted, but that emotion was not there. In comparison, what lifted me was my feeling the presence and action of people around me with the knowledge that people from all over were lifting me up in thought and prayer. Everything else seemed to be only words that carried no weight, regardless of the source. This was difficult for me to comprehend at the time.

After several days in my awakened stage, one morning I heard several nurses tell me, "You're a miracle man! You're a miracle man!" I was trying to digest that thought when they exclaimed, "The neurologist explained that you are recovering, and the reason is that you have the body of a forty-six-year-old man." I questioned the validity of that statement because it didn't make much sense to me at the time. I knew that many people forty-six years old and much younger have died of hemorrhagic strokes. I remembered a lovely young schoolgirl, a neighbor, who had died from that exact same cause. And I learned that a fifty-five-year-old man, who was admitted about the same time as I and for the same condition, unfortunately had died not long after being admitted. On the other hand, it was comforting to realize that I had entered the hospital at eighty-three years of age and now I was forty-six years old(?). Gosh, that was giving me some bragging rights. It later became apparent that the staff's "miracle man" description didn't take into consideration a final outcome without complications. And yet, the events that were to follow would indeed establish the reality of miracles.

THE CERTAINTY OF A
PROTECTIVE FORCE

My past medical history included having had a severe heart attack twenty-six years before, at the age of fifty-seven. After this, I had inquired of my cardiologist what steps I could take to prevent future attacks. It was distressing to hear him say that because of the damage to my heart, it was "too late for that now." My days were numbered? All life insurance was subsequently denied me. Six years later, a quadruple coronary bypass was complicated with a heart attack during the surgery. Excessive bleeding at the same time required a blood transfusion. That transfused blood began to destroy my blood cells. The hematocrit (packed cell volume) dropped to fifteen from a normal level of over forty. This meant that my blood volume had dropped to a third of its normal level. This required another transfusion with two units of blood. This new blood must have been of a different type, since my blood cells were no longer being destroyed.

Subsequently there were four more heart attacks and a series of nine coronary stent insertions and hospitalization with a severe case of double pneumonia, all over the next twenty-five years. These events seemed to indicate an eventual prognostic outcome of congestive heart failure, if not multiple organ failure. That would be if another heart attack didn't kill me. Yet, none of this took place. During this period of time, when I was seventy years of age, a PSA reading of twenty-three caused concern. My urologist stated that if prostate cancer was the reason for the elevated PSA, then I might not want to do anything about it because something else would probably kill me before the cancer. I asked, "How much time could I live with the cancer?"

He replied, "About ten years."

I said, "How about if I wanted to live twenty more years?" He revised his opinion by suggesting that maybe in that event, the cancer should be treated. As it turned out, there was no prostate cancer. There was a grossly enlarged prostate that required a TURP procedure to eliminate multiple catheterizations and/or hydronephrosis.

Throughout my life, I could feel the spirit of Jesus as being always with me. I never remember my having any specific prayers for recoveries. I trusted my life and wellbeing completely to the care of Jesus. Whatever the outcome, it would be all right, whether it be death or not. I had complete faith in His goodness and His guardianship. It was through a special spirit, which I identify as Jesus, that I had contact with God. My experiences have enabled me to believe in particular providence.

A MIRACLE IN THE COURT SYSTEM

A miraculous nonmedical event occurred in 1968 when I became the single father of four young children despite a Virginia court judge's final decision that I was never to see my two young daughters again. To the best of my knowledge, that decision has never been rescinded, and such a result, as far as I know, is unprecedented. My young daughters had been taken as far away as Scotland to live, and there, they were told that they would never see their father again. There was an urgent need to rescue them from their intolerable environment. Later, they would tell me that their constant prayer was that they would finally be united with their father. After a private detective's tip as to their whereabouts, the long-anticipated reunion finally took place in Springfield, Missouri, soon after they had arrived back to this country from Scotland. That situation was preceded by many charges and arrests connected with the endeavor of gaining the custody of my children over a period of more than a few years. Fortunately, I never spent so much as a night in jail, even though on several occasions, there were some close calls with many threats when facing contempt of court charges and charges of child abduction. Though I had lost every court battle regarding my children, the war for custody was won by extrajudicial means. The spirit of Jesus was with me, and the powerful judicial system did give way to that spiritual presence that interceded on my behalf.

Here are the four: Bill, Gregory, Missy, and Bunbun

RECOVERY FROM A
DEVASTATING TRAGEDY

This spiritual presence in my life has done more than facilitate miracles and near-miracles. My oldest son, Bill, was a precocious boy, extremely talented in art and deeply loved by his family. In 1973, at the age of twenty years old, Bill committed suicide. At that time, he was a student at St. Mary's College in Maryland.

His younger brother Greg was his roommate. Greg had just returned from being away for the weekend when he found his brother, Bill, hanging from his belt attached to a closet door.

I was awakened early on a Monday morning by the doorbell. I asked

Greg what he was doing home. He told me the very thing I had never wanted to hear: "Bill is dead." He says that his greatest fear was in having to tell me that Bill had died. It has been the very worst thing that has ever happened in my life. It is terrible to lose a child, especially when our children are expected to outlive their parents. Suicide presented the worst type of an unfathomable scenario.

Bill had been a patient at Johns Hopkins Phipps Hospital for about a year, where he had received treatment for severe depression. He had had a propensity for depression for several years before entering Phipps during his junior year in high school. After considerable improvement, Bill was able to leave, but not before taking and passing the GED examination, making him eligible for college entrance. As it turned out, he was able to enter college a year before he would have graduated from high school under normal conditions. He entered Saint Mary's College and became an excellent student, excelling in art. During his junior year there, his As began to turn into Bs. This appeared to have been precipitated by problems with his various girlfriends. This led to a depression that overwhelmed him; he couldn't live with it. His despondency led to suicide. Yet, knowing Bill, if he were capable of thinking rationally at the time, he would have never committed that act if he could have foreseen its tragic consequences. Severe deep depression is so overwhelming that suicide often appears to be the only relief from its destructive force. There has been an endowment scholarship fund established in his name at Saint Mary's College.

After this devastating news, how well I remember the times when I attempted to sleep at night while the most terrible dreams invaded my sleep. As I awoke, I was to realize that the events were much worse than any dream could produce. I wanted to die. Oh God, why did this have to happen? I trusted that answers would be forthcoming. I never lost faith in God. Finally, answers began to form. If my children ever had problems, no matter to what extent, Dad could always remedy the problems. There was nothing I couldn't take care of. Whoa, this was the one thing I could not fix. Here, I lacked control. I wasn't in total control after all. This was a difficult lesson to learn.

God was beginning to answer my questions. And from God's comforting presence, I knew that Bill's brother and sisters needed me badly, especially during that time of grieving. The spirit of the loving

God has continued to sustain me. Yet, the memory of that day and time period is always with me, frequently as if it were only yesterday. Now back to my anticipated recovery in the hospital.

Yes, things were going well in the hospital, and the unexpected was happening: I was improving to the point of an anticipated recovery while enjoying the status of being a "miracle man." However, one neurologist, with good reason, warned my daughters, "If he does recover, he'll never be the same again." I understand that the girls disputed that prognosis by saying, "You don't know my father." There is nothing like hope and faith against all odds.

One evening, Elaine decided that she would go home to get a good night's rest, with the confidence that her husband was doing so well in the process of a miraculous recovery. She had only been home several hours before receiving an urgent call from the hospital. Her husband had taken a sudden turn for the worse, and she needed to get back to the hospital right away. Was this request given in anticipation of his death?

During this time, an overwhelming pressure with extreme discomfort and an indescribable sensation took over my body to the point that it became absolutely unbearable. I needed an escape route. I could hear some of my children calling to me, "Dad, we need you. Dad, we need you." I could hear them but couldn't see them in my comatose condition. I felt complete exhaustion, which made it impossible for me to be energized in response to their pleas. They later affirmed their oral pleas at my bedside, but that moment appears to have taken place when I first arrived at the hospital in an unconscious state. Yet, these same voices were resonating in my mind as if in real time. Now it appears to have been a carryover from my initial experience shortly after arriving at Johns Hopkins Bayview. I realized at that time that those words were intended to encourage me to rally and continue to live. I remember appreciating those words so much, yet they were of no use; their value disappeared when that unbearable oppression initiated a determined action on my part to escape the malady that became so unbearable. The spark of life had left me, and my only recourse was to open that inviting door to death, which I could see right before me. It looked like a regular door with a gold-colored, round knob. I reached down to turn the knob so that I might enter the welcoming door of death. There was no fear, only an anticipated and welcomed relief from an unbearable burden. No other thought crossed my mind except that with a determined urgency which had never failed me, I needed to open that inviting door and find eternal and blessed relief. Even as I reached down to open the door, a period of unrecognizable time passed until the door was no longer there. Surprisingly, I was denied entry by the door's disappearance in spite of my most intensive efforts to pass through that portal. It was a great disappointment that the door to death was no longer available to me.

Awareness of time faded until the following morning, when I awoke to find myself feeling better. Elaine was at my side, and from her, I learned the reason for the urgent call she had received: I had developed double pneumonia, which was also a combination of both aspiration and bacterial pneumonia. As if this wasn't enough, I had also had a heart attack at the same time. There it was, the triple whammy, and yet I was still alive through all of this, despite my determined effort to escape this world by opening that welcoming door of death. In my mind, there was only one answer to the disappearance of the door and my recovery: divine intervention. This whole experience had unforeseeable consequences. When the door to death was denied me, another door opened.

REFLECTION

During the next week, my physical condition continued to improve. I finally reached the point of recovery when the next phase of hospitalization would be finalized (at much insistence on my part) with a stay at Kernan's Rehabilitation Center. I was admitted to Kernan's during the weekend, so there wasn't much activity going on there. However, a speech therapist was assigned to treat me. Why, I wondered, did I need a speech therapist? I thought my speaking ability was passable. It was then that I learned that the thrust of the therapist's treatment was to strengthen my swallowing reflex. This deficiency is what had caused the aspiration part of my pneumonia and had developed as a result of the stroke.

I grew frustrated with my treatment and determined that I should get home as soon as possible. A determined and reluctant nurse wanted to keep me much longer, but my insistence and persistence, communicated through Elaine, prompted the doctor to discharge me with his full consent.

I arrived at home and found I needed to use a walker, since my legs were so weak from disuse. Within a day or two, in being able to be up and exercise my legs, the pain in both my legs and back, which had burdened me so much in the hospital, had disappeared. It was a happy day when, much later, I was able to break into a short run.

A PENETRATING MESSAGE

From the totality of this whole misadventure with the miracle of divine intervention, a message penetrated my mind. I knew that I must share this with the world, about how my experience legitimized the existence of God and the available spiritual presence of Jesus. Then, too, the inaudible message from God, which showed the true path to be taken toward gaining a fully rewarding life and life's destiny, came through the action of loving all people, which leads to the knowledge of God.

Euphoria was seeping into my psyche, especially while sitting on the swing at my home, facing the driveway and the lawn with its grass, flowers, and trees. I could feel the vibrancy of life all around me. I heard the birds singing, watched them flying around, and inhaled the warm, fresh breeze that I likened to the breath of God. It was so simple, not at all complicated. Here I was absorbing the spirit of life that was all around me. The song of God seemed to envelope me. I loved everyone, everyone everywhere—with no restrictions! Singing and listening to songs of inspiration, especially many of the familiar hymns of my youth, brought a tranquility that only music can produce. I was flying high on the human spirit in complete freedom. Ah, there's heaven right here on earth. If there is a ladder to heaven, this is the first rung. I was reminded of Albert Schweitzer's philosophy, "Reverence for life." Life, what a wonderful gift! Everything was going my way: truly living life to the fullest, not just existing. Oh, the importance of people in my life! Those who are living, support life. The living things of all nature—animals, vegetation, and especially people—support and promote life. A strong impression swept over me to reveal that the pathway to God was found in people. Life without people and that interaction is like a swimming pool without water. Was that love of all people restricted to family, friends, Christians? No, it was love for all people, present and past, no matter what bad decisions they may have made in their lives. Yes, this love even included the likes of Stalin and Hitler. I loved everyone with no exception. This concept of complete love reminded me of the instructions from Jesus as found in the New Testament: Forgive and pray for your enemies, and also turn the other cheek. I was no longer a captive of ill feelings; I was free! It was as Jesus noted: "If you obey my commandments, you will know the truth, and the truth will set you free." This was a clear message that loving God was to be developed by loving people first; otherwise, it would be like putting the cart before the horse. That isn't meant to say that people are to be put first over the love of God, but that the love of God progresses from our love of people. God, whom no one can see, develops and expands through people whom we can see. It became clear to me that to love God was to love all people, a prerequisite to loving God.

Here was a type A personality resuscitated to live in the spirit of Jesus. Thus, I found what it was to really live, not merely to exist. This love required a constant and continuous practice. Any interruption in this practice of continuous love gave way to compromising a continuing pure happiness. As time went on over the next several months, kinks started to develop in my armor. The euphoria, which I had envisioned as a permanent fixture, would disappear, and that pendulum could swing the other way.

Much has been written on how to obtain happiness, its origin, and its implementation. The *Johns Hopkins Magazine*, fall 2010 issue, has an excellent article on the pursuit of happiness with contributions from many people on the subject of what makes them happy. To me, experiencing the love for all people, and consequently for God, formed the basis for my newfound happiness, even with its peaks and valleys. This love becomes a constant upon which happy moments can build. Separate events and situations that produce happy experiences tend to be transient, yet produce more euphoria when they surface on the background of the infinite love, here described.

Deviation from the constant, ongoing love had a direct bearing on the happiness that I otherwise experienced. Those kinks were brought on by my failure, on occasion, to turn the other cheek, so that unqualified love lost its hold. Malice and hostility, often experienced by type A personalities, become great enemies of the tranquility and the peace of mind that radiate from the background of love. I discovered that a real working effort was required on my part for my actions and reactions to be completely consistent with the spirit of love. One of my life's biggest challenges was the effort to overcome the selfishness that is an inherent enemy of love. Overcoming difficult tasks has its rewards. Finding and experiencing the truth reach the pinnacle of tranquility.

Do not all people have one commonality as members of the human race? Did that love include homosexuals? Absolutely. Stereotyping on that subject disappeared from my mind years ago. After I was discharged from the navy in 1946, the Frederick Presbyterian Church, where I was a member, decided that it would be good if the young war veterans were put to use as ushers. One of my fellow ushers was John, whom I only knew as one of the sons of my favorite Sunday school teacher. Through the next several years, I acquired an admiration and respect for John. He was about four years older than I, a college graduate, working as an engineer. I always admired intelligence, and that was John, who was also one of the nicest persons I had ever known. We remained casual acquaintances throughout the time I knew him. In 1951, I married my first wife in Richmond, Virginia. I hadn't invited John to the wedding, but he showed up anyway and brought us a very nice present. I was both surprised and grateful. About three years later, when I was at the University of Georgia, I heard that he had died. The rumor was that he had committed suicide because he found himself to have homosexual tendencies. He was a deeply religious person, and with the Christian church's view on homosexuality, it was a complex situation that he could not live with. This was in the early 50s, when societal standards were much more rigid than they are today. That hurt me so much, as it still deeply hurts me today. John had those uncontrollable feelings that gave him a huge sense of guilt that wasn't compatible with life in the society of which he was a member. Those feelings were deeply embedded, even though not acted out. This was such a tragic loss for his family and friends. It shouldn't require a personal experience like this to have compassion in situations of this nature.

Did this love of all people extend to violent criminals that fill our news channels daily? Yes. Praying for those who have ruined the lives of others and their own lives by making bad decisions aids the forgiver by preventing therein a mind filled with hostility, which would have been another victim. After having spent more than three years in prison ministry, I came to realize that the inmates were no different from you or me, only to the extent of their having made more destructive decisions. There was still that commonality of life and the potential for a life dedicated to a common good.

The thrust of uplifting people is a constructive endeavor that supports life and the enjoyment of life. Tearing down people is a selfish and destructive effort that is a one-way street to sadness and a debilitating cancer of the psyche. Can we build ourselves up by tearing down others? Selfishness supports that thought.

It is so easy to stereotype. All Muslims are evil? All Christians are hypocrites? All Americans are corrupt? It goes on and on. That trap of erroneous thinking can be avoided by making an effort to personally know members of all of these different groups. That procedure could have modified the great Gandhi's thoughts when he declared that "I like your Jesus. I do not like your Christians. Your Christians are so unlike your Christ." Here, Gandhi also stereotyped by voicing an opinion directed toward a religious group based upon his experience with a large number, but not all, who walked under the banner of "Christian." Still, Gandhi's whole life was spent in the pursuit of truth, a noble endeavor.

My experience in associating with many members of the stereotyped groups has led to the insight that we all have so much in common. No group or person will determine for me what my opinion should be of others. That would be through my personal experience alone. I would never allow that brainwashing control in my life, such as that which happened to the followers of Jim Jones, who led nine hundred people to their deaths. There appear to be a lot of Jim Joneses in this world, leading many people astray.

PASTORAL CARE

Shortly after my having arrived at home from the hospital, an opportunity to help and to fortify people was opened to me in the form of the pastoral care program at the Howard County General Hospital.

The Howard County General Hospital sponsors a volunteer group that provides spiritual support for hospital patients. The volunteers come with many different religious identities but do not promote their beliefs to the patients. The sole focus is to uplift those who are hospitalized. It presents a wonderful opportunity to help others. Yet an amazing consequence of this endeavor is that the giver of comfort and encouragement also becomes the receiver. I presently visit every Thursday evening. The rapport and the kindred spirits that result from these visits lift me to emotional highs on these evenings. I'm so energized afterwards that even my appetite for food is greatly stimulated. The downside is that when it comes to food, I then tend to violate that ancient axiom of "moderation in all things." Life is so great!

This whole experience has been a special blessing to me. Each patient is very unique. All visits result in an appreciation for human bonding and reveal how much we really need each other. My visits are also very educational. One patient gave me her experience in the hospital that I found to be of great value. She was such a nice lady, in her sixties. We developed an instant rapport. During the course of our conversation, she related her experience at the hospital when she was a patient the previous spring. She was having trouble breathing at the time. After she complained to a person she identified as a technician in her room, the technician's response was, "Take a deep breath." She did so, but continued having difficulty in breathing. In desperation, she dialed 911. The 911 operator asked for her location, so she responded with her room number in the hospital and complained that she wasn't getting help. This kindly lady then told me that right after she hung up from the 911 call, hospital personnel started rushing into her room. They found that she had fluid building up in her lungs, ultimately resulting in her condition being successfully treated. The moral of that story is, if you are a patient in a hospital and can't get help for a dire need, dial 911.

Another patient described a near-death experience that she had had several years previously. She was seriously ill and found herself diving into a pool of emerald-green water. As she descended, she was given two options: either she could continue that journey to death or she could return to the living state. She chose to return to the living state, yet it was not an easy decision to make. She experienced the message that if she had chosen death, there would be no judgment associated with that experience. Previous to that, she had been a member of the Church of Christ. She was awakened by this spiritual revelation and appeared to have abandoned what was thought to be the misinformation propagated by mainline Christian churches.

It seems that of the patients I visit, at least half of that number no longer claim membership in any organized religious churches. They claim spirituality, but profess disillusionment with their previous affiliation.

THE MESSAGE

Was my experience with Jesus, the spiritual messenger from God, due to the accident of my birth into a Christian family? Was I special in this respect? Are the Jews of the Old Testament special as being recorded by the writers of the Bible as those chosen by God from all the peoples of the earth? Is the vindictive God of fury, as recorded in the Old Testament, compatible with the loving God presented by Jesus in the New Testament?

Does the secret to a full and rewarding life and a spiritual connection to God require the belief and faith in a triune God? Are all other religious beliefs excluded? Muslims believe that the unforgiveable sin is to believe that God has a partner, as in Jesus Christ, whereas the Christian church believes that salvation is only available to those who believe that Jesus Christ is part of a Triune God. Could it be that the God of the universe is so lacking in self-esteem and so easily intimidated that this almighty God resorts to the human traits of selfishness and jealousy in order to maintain legalistic legitimacy? Here again, man has described God as made in the image of man, with all of man's foibles. How could an inquiring mind accept this concept of such a little God that reveals all of the weaknesses shared with man? God is not in a box. The true God is far above the pettiness of man and stands over the feeble gods invented by man. The all-loving God, revealed by Jesus, appears to be a most potent God, rising to the highest level that is unattainable by man, while possessing none of the foibles of man. This wonderful love dissolves fear. The true God is the God of many religions, in spite of not being recognized as such, even by the mainline Christian churches.

I received the clear and convincing message that there is God, a God of general providence who gave nature its laws to be exercised by nature alone. That same God is also a God of particular providence, which is exercised by God through spiritual messenger(s). I have felt the presence of the one I identify as Jesus and the benefit of His spirit being with me for many years. The results of His spiritual presence in my life have previously given me the hint of ongoing miracles. The actual occurrence of miracles in this event is well-documented here.

The only requirement for this full life and experiencing the presence of God is to first love people, all people. When the path of loving all people is followed, God will be found. Unfortunately there are often roadblocks. Malice, hostility, and hate for anyone form a detour on the road to God. Those taking that detour invalidate any claim to legitimacy as to a relationship with God. Self-centeredness and arrogance produce the malice and hate that replace that valuable experience of love. Love is an essential ingredient in knowing God and living a full and wonderful life. The experience of love and malice cannot coexist. One replaces the other. Having spent too much time with the ugly spirit of malice in my life, I can attest to its destructive and valueless nature.

That outrageous arrogance found in hubris exists as the great enemy in the spirit of mankind. History validates this assertion. This characteristic was made quite evident in the lives of many religious leaders, including John Calvin and Martin Luther. It continues to this day in the Christian world. This characteristic is to be found in all religious endeavors and in every walk of life. Stalin and Hitler are names synonymous with hubris. It would be good for each of us to recognize the destructive results of outrageous arrogance, as it tends to creep into our own lives. To avoid selfishness is to avoid hubris in our lives.

The love of God, the action of which is manifested by doing that which is right and in loving all people, results in complete integrity. That action also leads to a clear conscience. The absence of a clear conscience is made whole by revisiting our mistakes and becoming completely aligned with the presence of God in our hearts. The act of loving people, all people, with no exceptions, is of equal importance. Equal? Yes, for without this harmony of people in our lives, God is impotent. This is implied in the words of Jesus concerning God and the need for loving and forgiving all people. Jesus plainly states that our sins are not forgiven unless we forgive others.

The clear message is that those who totally practice this absolute love for God and mankind will receive the same results, whether or not by professed Christians, those of other religions, or even those who may deny a religious conviction. They will be practicing the commandments of Christ, knowingly or not. This is the essence of Jesus' answer to the teacher of the law, as found in Luke 10:25, when that Pharisee inquired of Jesus, "What shall I do to inherit eternal life?" Then, why was Jesus born? John 18:37 tells us that Jesus said that he was born for the purpose of revealing the truth. The truth that Jesus revealed was that love was superior to tradition. Tradition was supporting the misguided beliefs among His fellow Jews, as it continues today among many religious groups. Tradition without the overriding theme of love becomes a great imposter of "truth."

It follows that any religion or religious belief that advocates and supports the elimination of life by killing people challenges the providence of God and thus condemns itself as the enemy of God and subsequently the enemy of all mankind. Is the "Right to Life" movement limited to preserving life before birth? After birth, is it all right to advocate situations where life is put at risk by sending adults to conflicts where they are butchered and brought back in body bags? Is there not obviously hypocrisy in this position? Yet the advocates give themselves plenty of wiggle room that falls flat on its face when scrutinized with the spirit of Christ as its cornerstone. The etiology of these destructive beliefs and actions comes from the exercise of selfishness, with its developing hubris. This characterization can apply to governments that identify themselves as theocracies and to those governments that act as theocracies but characterize themselves otherwise. Gandhi has observed and noted that, "The only people on earth who do not see Jesus and His teachings as nonviolent are Christian." Of course, that is a general impression, as many Christians do see nonviolence as a permeating characteristic of Christianity. The Society of Friends is one such entity.

Gandhi's other reported quotes are worthy of consideration and contemplation: "An eye for an eye makes the whole world blind." "There are many causes I am prepared to die for, but no causes I am prepared to kill for." "The Truth is more important than any weapon of mass destruction." "As soon as we lose the moral basis, we cease to be religious. There is no such thing as religion overriding morality. Man, for instance, cannot be untruthful, cruel, or incontinent and claim to have God on his side." And in recognizing himself as a member of the human race, when Gandhi was asked if he was a Hindu, he replied, "Yes, I am. I am also a Christian, a Muslim, a Buddhist, and a Jew." Therein lay a general commonality, if not a specific commonality. Do not his observations have a ring of truth?

In the Old Testament, writers show their God to be vindictive, vacillating, resentful, possessed with malice, capable of fury, and to be greatly feared. Hence, the "fury of God" was invented. When "God's people" were in the process of making a land-grab, the writers had God commanding Saul to kill all of the Amalekites and to destroy all of their animals. Saul seems to have had more compassion than God when he spared some. And God was furious with Saul and punished him for not obeying His directive. That same theme and fallacious assumption of a vindictive God have fueled the corruption of the Christian religion. They have sponsored the corruption of the growing Christian church when heretics were tortured by being burned at the stake and also gave validity for the Inquisition and the cruelty of the Crusades. That God, envisioned by the Old Testament writers, seems to have been made in the image of man with all of man's faults. That message survives in the form of tradition. It is in contradiction to the all-loving God that Jesus espoused.

Unfortunately, the violence in the Old Testament seems to have been carried over into the mentality of the Christian church after Emperor Constantine legalized Christianity by the Edict of Milan in 313 AD. Shortly after the controversy between Athanasius, who supported homoousios (of the same substance as God), and Arius, who supported homoiousios (of a similar nature as God), the theological differences ended with Athanasius prevailing when a minority of the bishops in the Roman empire voted for Athanasius' position of homoousios at the First Ecumenical Council at Nicaea in 325 AD. Those who supported the Arius position were banished from the Roman empire. Just as Arius was to be readmitted to the orthodox Christian community by the order of Emperor Constantine, he met an agonizing death at the hands of his "Christian" enemies. Good circumstantial evidence indicated that his "Christian" adversaries provided for his demise. From then on, persecution of those with different theologies slowly materialized, but escalated after Emperor Theodosius made Christianity the official religion of the Roman empire in 380 AD. Heretics were welcomed as enemies of orthodoxy to be persecuted by the most violent means available.

Does the Old Testament have value? Yes, it does. Many parts, such as Psalms and Proverbs, can be very inspirational, and it should be noted that this part of the Old Testament is found in the small Bible edition distributed by the Gideons International.

Does God judge us after we die? The strong message that I had received is that God does not judge, much less put us into hell. We judge ourselves as we continue life's journey, and when we die, we continue into death with the same spiritual journey, even as to the hell of our own making or that heaven of our own making. We have already judged our destiny in death by living a selfish life or an unselfish life. The path we follow in life continues past the Door of Death.

A dangerous misconception based on misinformation is that Jesus paid the price for our sins and all are saved through their faith that Jesus is God. Those who believe thus have their sins forgiven and then gain entrance into heaven. The very spirit of Jesus contradicts this perception. Jesus' requisite of the love He promoted through His commandments cannot be overridden by the slippery slope of automatic forgiveness and faith alone. Matthew 7:22-24 alerts the misguided that magic words are not sufficient.

A REBIRTH EXPERIENCE

My life became like a born-again experience, with a new body and a new mind—new in the sense that the new me was a resounding improvement over the old me. Physically, the top of my head began growing hair where there had been no hair for years. The sensation of my heart and my body having been seriously compromised, as was present prior to this stroke, had disappeared.

I wanted and expected this euphoria to last forever. Not! Later, I was to find that any interruption in this experience was funded by the absence of complete and total love. As the days passed, that euphoria began to be interrupted by the advancing despair of depression, a reminder of my life-long propensity for depression. I couldn't understand this transition. Then came the day when I felt the spark of life disappearing. It became a one-way spiral toward the feeling of death. But on that very day, many members of the Howard Hitters, a softball team with whom I played, decided to visit me and to celebrate my coming home. How well I remember their presence lifting me up and encouraging me. My friend John Cress called me the "iron man" for having survived. They presented me with a softball that had been signed by all of the team members. They really cared! That enabled the spark to suddenly burst into the flame of life once more

I told them right then, "You have just saved my life, though I don't expect you to understand what I am saying." I began to discover the cause of that unanticipated despair. It was just too easy for me to fall back into old habits. The ever-present negative news from the news media and so many negative political email attachments seemed to have taken hold of my brain. My love for all people was invaded and compromised by this psychic enemy.

The nudge of this experience validated that very clear spiritual message that I had received. The road to eternal life is reached by traveling the road of life paved by the love for all people. We can experience heaven while we are living on earth until the very time and place when our physical bodies cease to live. This heaven on earth and heaven after death are available to all who practice Jesus' love commandments and their ramifications. There are those who never heard of Jesus and those who don't share the traditional creeds of modern Christianity. Makes no difference; creeds won't do it. The key to the good life now, as we approach the afterlife of heaven, is only to be found in the practice of loving all people and in revering all life. Sole reliance on a deeply entrenched tradition often becomes a major roadblock on the road to eternal life and to the truly found happiness while we live on this earth.

As the next few days developed, I learned from Elaine that my name had been on prayer chains involving thousands of people. It extended all the way to Thailand. It seemed, at the same time, that I felt the rush of people as if it were a flowing river of people elevating me from the depths of death to the excitement of a life previously unknown. Could that feeling be a result of particle physics, where the message was traveling through space on the back of neutrinos, which penetrate our bodies many times a second, or of some other weak force of nature like the subatomic particle bosons?

On the subject of science, theoretical physicists believe that there are at least two impossibilities in science. One impossibility is the ability to produce absolute zero, and the other impossibility is the ability to create a perpetual motion device. Though many may speculate on the scientific impossibly of recognizing the entity of God, that door is still open. I firmly believe that, sooner, if not later, we'll recognize that the spiritual world and the world of physics are more closely intertwined than has been believed. It will be learned that science and religion support each other and can work together and that the true spirit of God embraces both subjects. As Albert Einstein once said, "Science without religion is lame; a religion without science is blind."

From that moment of gathered insight about the importance of people and on how we are helped to live through constructive interaction with people, I started on the road to being the happiest that I had ever been in my life. The neurologist was correct; I would never be the same again, yet there were no deficits, only the most positive of positives.

From the medical standpoint, having survived that massive stroke, the resulting damage to my brain should have produced hydrocephalus, with subsequent seizures and ultimate cognitive deficiencies. That happiness developed as my continuous search for truth exploded before me. The truth for the ultimate life was being realized. The pieces of that puzzle were beginning to form the picture of an ultimate truth. This truth was illuminated by the realization that people were the vehicle that provided the matrix. I loved all people, everyone. No one was an exception. That wonderful feeling enveloped me. That love extended to Joseph Stalin, Hitler, and murderers. These were people, yet in spite of their bad deeds, the fact that they were living beings carried a certain element of good. There was no more resentment in my life, no more hostility. Whatever grievance I had for anyone in the past was now gone. No one had the ability to make me angry. I was really free, as Jesus had promised. I thought that if everyone in the world felt this way, there would be no wars and no crime, only peace on earth and goodwill toward everyone. I couldn't be responsible for all people, but I could be responsible for me. I knew that it was necessary for me to uplift people, just as people have elevated me. What a glorious position to experience! The assumption was that this elation would last forever. As time went on, this experience would be revisited many times. I felt the strong desire, in fact a mandate, to share all of this with the rest of world by writing a book. Fortunately, I dallied and waited a year before writing about these events. Passage of time has validated that procrastination.

Two weeks after I arrived home, a CT scan was scheduled at Johns Hopkins Bayview Medical Center to determine if the remaining blood in and around my brain was being absorbed. The neurologist appeared to be surprised at my agile mobility. I was asked about how many seizures I had experienced. (Not if I had had any; obviously the presumption was that I had,) When I responded, "None," I noted a look of surprise.

Over the next two months, two more scans were scheduled, and on the last scan, all of the remaining blood had been reabsorbed. Good news! Everything was going my way and would continue to do so as long as I followed Jesus' commandments and their ramifications: loving God and loving all people in the spirit of Jesus, with no exceptions. Security, you are mine.

Although I attribute my survival to divine intervention and a spiritual presence of Jesus being with me through my illness that was finalized by that door to death being closed, I appreciate so much the caring experience of the Howard County General Hospital emergency crew and at Johns Hopkins Bayview. At the Bayview Medical Center, I was even privileged to be under the care of a nurse who was a client of the Everhart Animal Hospital. She came in with a special dedication to give me optimal care. I well remember her lecturing me about my stubbornness for my continuous attempts to remove my arm restraints.

As it turned out, I had experienced **three miracles**. The **first miracle** was certainly in the eyes of the Bayview staff, when they called me the "miracle man" for having survived the initial massive brain bleed characterized by a grave prognosis supported by the CT scan. My family, both medical and non-medical, concurred.

The **second miracle** was the moment of the event when death was denied me, in spite of my insistence toward that end, as complications of a simultaneous heart attack and double pneumonia were ready to end my life. That event, with its overwhelming and indescribable oppression, prompted my determined effort to open the door of death. Yet, I wasn't allowed to die when that door disappeared to become no longer available. Was that not divine intervention and a miracle?

The **third miracle** was the new physical and mental life that I experienced. There were no physical or mental deficits resulting from the life-threatening physical damage from that misadventure, despite the prognosis to the contrary. To the contrary, this was a new life, a new beginning, both mentally and physically, like being born again. Several months after I arrived home, my primary care physician, Dr. Scott Mauer, gave me a thorough examination. He reported that there was no evidence that I had ever had a stroke. Except for the medical records, he would never have known about the stroke!

My body was experiencing the greatest health boost it had ever known. The physical damage had completely reversed it self. As stated previously, hair was now growing on the bald spots of my head. I may never have a full head of hair, but that was a beginning, easily recognized by my family. My heart seemed to be experiencing renewed vitality, inherited heart disease genes and heart damage from many previous heart attacks notwithstanding. This became quite evident during the blizzard the following January, when the Baltimore region experienced record snowfalls. Snow had accumulated to a depth of over three feet in a four-day period. Over the following week, I shoveled snow eight to ten hours a day in order to clear my rather large driveway. The ability to do that would have been impossible before the stroke. Now, however, my body felt really good, without a hint of chest discomfort. The sensation of my heart and my body having been seriously compromised, which was present prior to this stroke, had disappeared. I told Elaine that if I continued shoveling snow, my arms would soon be larger than my legs. In fact, muscle was growing there. Many months later, when my cardiologist learned about my snow-shoveling experience, I thought he was going to have a heart attack. He was emphatic in stating that I should never be shoveling snow, even after my telling him about how great it had made me feel. He fortified his position by telling me that two of his clients had died from heart attacks as a result of shoveling snow during that same period. My argument to the contrary, that one size didn't fit all, got nowhere. In one sense, he was right, because from the practice of medicine standpoint, any advice to the contrary under the circumstances would have been tantamount to malpractice. However, it seems that the practice of medicine doesn't allow for the intervention of miracles.

My ability to handle that strenuous activity was largely due to a different mental outlook and the peace of mind that was mine. At last I had seemed to have found that ultimate truth which I had long pursued, a knowledge that was plainly available to me before, but hidden behind those all-too-common human traits of selfishness and misinformation. The truth revealed was the validity of Jesus' basic commandments: "If you obey my commandments, you will know the truth, and the truth will set you free." The New Testament states that Jesus told Pontius Pilate that he was born to reveal the truth. Then, when a teacher of the law, a Pharisee, asked Jesus what he must do to find everlasting life, Jesus asked him, "What do the scriptures tell you?"

The Pharisee answered, "Love God with all of your heart, all of your mind, and all of your strength, and love your neighbor as yourself."

Jesus answered, "You answered well; do that and you will live." Live! Not only to inherit eternal life, but live (really live a full and abundant life). Those commandments of loving, forgiving, and praying for your enemies and turning the other cheek left no place in the emotions for anything else except for a love that called for action. Malice in any form and under any condition is to be replaced by love. Malice and love do not coexist in the spirit of God or in the godly. I repeat: no one and no event could make me angry. Loving God also calls for action, the action of always doing the right thing, personifying absolute integrity. Anything else is found in words alone. Only action speaks where words fail. These actions required their being followed completely and in their entirety. I have long been aware of these words, yet my actions in carrying out those commandments were sporadic.

Now these words took on a different meaning. Action here was required every wakeful and sleep-filled minute. Only when I'm in complete compliance do I experience that perfect peace and happiness. In addition, I found that another ingredient was required: people, with whom a positive interaction produces a field of energized energy. The more people, the better. This can be likened to an automobile's engine, where more horsepower produces better performance. People are the matrix for carrying out these commandments. The process and life itself without people would indeed be like a swimming pool without water.

It doesn't take much scrutiny to question that a commonly accepted qualification for being a Christian is to believe in Jesus as part of the triune God. It is so easy to be identified as a Christian on that basis alone. That concept was absent from the revelation that I had received. The word *Christian* comes from the Greek word *Christianos*, meaning follower of Christ. A person can follow Jesus side by side and step by step or many miles behind. Miles behind allows for many distracting obstacles to interfere with Jesus' presence. Immediately following Jesus allows no room for interfering missteps. The result is that all of Jesus' commandments are followed exactly. There is no allowance for following closely occasionally. For most of my life, I have followed Jesus at a distance, obeying His commandments on loving God and loving people with all that was implied, as my mood permitted. My own selfishness, with its hostile, unforgiving, and critical nature, separated me from the perfect assimilation that I now find necessary to be identified as a Christian. Can a person be a Christian partially or most of the time without being fully committed and completely following Jesus' basic commandments all of the time? Can a woman be just a little bit or partially pregnant? To me, the ultimate Christian, who is the only Christian worthy of that identity, is one who maintains an ongoing obedience to Jesus' commandments that were given to the "teacher of the law," e.g., unqualified love for everyone. As Jesus went around doing good, so does any true follower of Jesus.

Everything began to go my way because hostility disappeared as my master. The outrageous arrogance of hubris, materialism, "will to power," and resentment all evaporated from my psyche. The consequence of this action of following the basic commandments from Jesus brought complete freedom, peace of mind, and happiness. Yes, an experience of heaven here on earth. With the knowledge that no one could make me angry and no resentment and hostility to raise my cortisol level, my physical heart rejoiced. The symptoms of the longstanding cardiovascular disease disappeared.

It appears to me that these words of Jesus, in this context, may not be limited to Christians or to the Christian religion. That same theme may be found in many other religions, and the same results can be obtained from its practice. Which of these two men showed the greatest Christian spirit: Winston Churchill, who called himself a Christian while condemning Gandhi as that Indian fakir who would never wrest India from the British Empire, or Gandhi? Well, Gandhi did free India, and he did so without using physical force, as in the spirit of Christ. While Churchill relied on physical force, with the weight of the mighty British military on his side, he was defeated by that "Indian fakir" who practiced the virtues of the Christian spirit as the pathway to his victory.

Inclusive here is the knowledge that loving all people is paramount. Encouraging others, just as people have encouraged me. Two other facets complete the fulfillment of complete happiness and living life to the fullest: One is in taking care of the physical body by doing nothing to harm it and by increasing the body's vitality through a nurturing life style. That includes exercising the muscles of the body that require exercise for optimum health, eating the right foods in the right proportions, and avoiding all harmful physical practices and substances. The second is in gaining knowledge and maintaining a continuously open mindset in seeking the truth in any avenue as it may develop. A closed mind is like a stone, whose only destiny is to turn into sand. Again, hubris is the great enemy of the Christian spirit.

My encounter in wishing for death and having it denied resulted in the gain of complete confidence and the fear of nothing. My whole mental outlook had changed. Insight into the meaning of life showed that that which I had considered before to be so important, particularly from a materialistic standpoint, was no longer important, but essentially meaningless and even a detriment to enjoying life.

I consider that, in spite of my act of insistent determination to open the door of death and having it denied me, established the circumstance for divine intervention. For most of my life, I have felt that Jesus, a spiritual messenger of God, was within me; that my faith in Jesus and His presence defined our relationship. And it was through Jesus that I appealed for the knowledge of truth, a lifelong quest that appears to have been largely finalized shortly after my having turned eighty-three years of age. Do I now have a closed mind? A closed mind closes the door to the entrance of truth. My mind will always be open for the spirit of truth to enter.

Yet, in spite of having experienced this great euphoria and acknowledging the reason for it from time to time, I eventually sank into a depression that simply confused me. All of my life, I have had the tendency to get depressed occasionally for no apparent reason. The depressed state shouldn't be happening to me now that I had found the true source of happiness. Right before my eyes, I discovered that I had fallen into a trap of my own making. My own hubris again was defining me as bulletproof. I could eat anything, especially the sweets I had long craved, yet maybe not. My exercise routine energized me with an increase of testosterone. That, in turn, encouraged a spirit of aggression with a side order of hostility. Nietzsche's "will to power" slowly invaded my psyche. I kept up with all of the latest news from the media, which implanted a downward spiral. The negative political emails I received also caused resentment in me. All of these poisoned the purity of a spiritual relationship. In order for me to be saturated with the harmony of happiness, it demanded perfect compliance, as in a love for all people under any circumstances. There was no room for me to be offended by anyone or anything to the extent of being controlled by that emotion. For me to be saturated with the harmony of happiness, the solution was self-control, kicking hubris out the door, eating the right foods, and totally immersing my psyche in those basic commandments of Jesus. With that, truth prevails. Still, as time goes on, immediate kneejerk reactions due to negative stimuli occasionally interrupt this tranquility. But now, when it occurs, it's a momentary interruption, soon forgotten. Practicing forgiveness progresses to promoting goodwill. The challenge is to diminish or eliminate the kneejerk in order to achieve continuous tranquility and euphoria.

SLIGHT HEMORRHAGE?

One day toward the end of June in 2010, I saw a friend of mine who remarked about my "slight hemorrhage" that I had suffered the previous year. That statement surprised me, since he was with a men's fellowship group with whom I had shared the miracle of that catastrophic event. He must have thought that I had grossly overstated and exaggerated my story of the massive brain bleed and the subsequent heart attack and pneumonia. And yet, I began to understand the reason for that assumption because my recovery gave no hint of my ever having had a stroke! My mind and my physical agility seemed to be better than ever, and it was as if I had been reborn to a new life. That was the part of me that my friend saw. To him, it obviously could have only been a slight stroke and slight hemorrhage.

This experience motivated me to put all doubt to rest. My life now becomes an open book. So for any interested person, on request, I waive any right to privacy that HIPAA grants me. My medical records are available to anyone. The only restriction is on any information that could be used for identity theft, such as my social security number and credit card numbers. In addition and just as important, there were those who were there when I went to the emergency room and on to the Bayview Medical Center who are willing to be interviewed as to what they observed and witnessed: my wife, Elaine; her friend, Barbara Himes, retired schoolteacher and deacon in the Rolling Hills Baptist Church; Dr. Greg Kang, my son-in-law and a physical medicine physician, who has a pain, spine, and sports practice in Myrtle Beach; my children, Gregory Everhart, Joy Kang (nurse), Carolyn Inman (nurse anesthesiologist), and April Woodall (veterinary assistant). To any doubters as to the true miracles in my life, I invite inquiry to disprove or substantiate their existence. Truth is the goal.

WHERE IT ALL BEGAN

The above-mentioned weren't the only miracles in my life. It all started on a journey I had begun many years before. This search for the truth began soon after my joining the navy at the age of seventeen, during World War II. My parents had raised me attending the Presbyterian Church in Frederick. I considered myself to be a Christian. Yet, in some of my discussions with my shipmates, religion often was the subject of debate. One discussion involved an avowed atheist, a Roman Catholic, and me, the Protestant. I was surprised to find a lot of animosity shown by my Roman Catholic friend toward my position as a fellow Christian. This was elevated to the extent that my Catholic friend was even taking the position of the atheist against the Protestant side. Okay, who is right? What is the truth? Because I was brought up to believe what I believed, how did that make it the right path to follow? The atheist had his upbringing, and the Roman Catholic had his. Consider the Muslim, the Buddhist, and the Hindu. Which path is right?

That question started me on my search for truth with the realization that only in an open mind would truth be realized. Clearly, tradition was the basis for the different religious beliefs.

TRADITION?

learned at the age of ten that tradition alone could not be depended upon to represent the truth. At that time, I considered my father as the wisest of men. This was in 1936, when there was racial segregation in my hometown of Frederick, Maryland. Since schools were not integrated, there was no opportunity to associate with anyone of a different race. There were colored (the classification of that time) boys who walked home from school, following the trolley tracks in front of my house. One day, some of my friends and I decided to throw stones at them, for no particular reason. That experiment didn't last long, because we soon found that they could throw harder and more accurately than we could.

That prompted me to inquire of my father, "Daddy, what's the difference between colored people and ourselves?"

Instead of answering directly, here the smartest person in the world asked me a question: "Do you think that you are better than they are?"

My considered conclusion was, "No, I don't think that I'm better than they are."

I wasn't ready for his next statement: "Of course you are."

"Of course" made absolutely no sense to me at all. Then, for the first time in my life, I came to realize that my father didn't have all of the answers to life's questions. My father had come from Northern Virginia, and he was well educated in the fallacy of his belief of racial superiority without having given it any independent thought. Subsequent experiences have verified the truth of my position. Some of the most intelligent, capable, and kind people I have had the privilege of knowing are African Americans. And such is my closest friend outside of my family, Sarah, who has always been in my corner and who was especially helpful when

I was a single parent of four young children. Tradition, standing alone, is not intrinsically the truth, nor does it legitimize its objective.

Is the tradition of a religion superior to a personal experience that could compromise a traditional belief? The Bible's New Testament validates the superiority of religious experience. Consider the story of Paul, a Pharisee, whose faith was based on tradition. He played a leading role in persecuting the early Christians. Subsequently he had the Damascus road experience, which led to his becoming the great defender of Christ.

Logical reasoning suggested to me that faith is not intrinsically the same as truth. Several hundred years ago, the Christian church had faith that the sun revolved around the earth, and there were severe consequences for believing otherwise. We now know, and the church acknowledges, that there was no truth in that belief. As with tradition, faith alone does not legitimize its objective.

Consequently, faith that one religious belief is the only true belief and that nonbelievers should be put to death prevailed for many hundreds of years in the Christian church, as well as in other religions. Now many of the organized Christian churches, lacking the support of the state, no longer burn heretics at the stake. Since that remedy no longer exists, heretics are now condemned to be burned in hell after death. Hmmm?

From this experience with my father, I knew that I needed to think for myself without depending on anyone for an ultimate answer. That began my search for the truth in everything, wherever it would take me. My ultimate goal in life was to find the truth. I used my Christian background as a basis to search for the truth through the use of prayer and an open mind. I had already experienced the presence of a spiritual world, though I was not sure of its dimensions. I believed in God and in Jesus and His teachings. Yet, if truth revealed that there was no God, I would have to accept it, although I very much hoped that it wouldn't be so. I knew that a closed mind closed the pathway to truth. This quest began the philosophy for my life and has brought me up to the present day. My conclusion rests on having examined the Bible through the years as a Sunday School teacher and a member of many Protestant churches and on gaining knowledge of Christianity's history. Yet, by far, the most important and conclusive evidence is my personal experience with God through Jesus' spiritual presence in my life through many years. The event of my stroke and convincing evidence of divine intervention necessitated this writing in order to reveal the true spirit of Christ revealed to me through this experience.

The ongoing search for truth has led me to the conclusion that there is a God, a loving God with spiritual messengers. The God that I know is similar to a CEO who delegates authority. God has created nature with its laws. Thus natural occurrences are not through the direct work of God. Those bad events that we experience in life are not the result of God's fury or maliciousness. God does not cause cancer, sickness, death, destructive storms, and catastrophic events. Most, if not all, religions that entertain a belief in God put their belief in an egocentric God, an entity that mimics human nature. This God, a great invention of human imagination, fades away when an awareness and knowledge of the God of the universe is revealed. There is no egocentricity in this spirit of inconceivable dimensions. Yet, it is a spirit that possesses divine providence and allows particular providence through at least one special messenger spirit. My experience, and perhaps the experience of many others, can verify the validity of this concept. This may be revealed only under special circumstances, such as in the state of death's aftermath or from a state of death denied. The one special messenger spirit that I have known is that spirit I identify as Jesus.

The nature of God represented in the Old Testament was contradicted by the teachings of Jesus, who, at the very least, becomes a very special spiritual agent of God. He taught that God is synonymous with love and that we should love people, turn the other cheek, and forgive everyone. The New Testament states that Jesus said to Pilate that he, Jesus, was born to reveal the truth. In Luke 10:25, a teacher of the law, a Pharisee, asked Jesus what he must do to inherit eternal life. Jesus asked him, "What do the scriptures tell you?"

The Pharisee answered, "Love God with all of you heart, all of your mind, and all of your strength, and love your neighbor as yourself."

Jesus answered, "You answered well; do that and you will live." Live! Not only to inherit eternal life but live (really live a full and abundant life). The commandments of forgiving and praying for your enemies and turning the other cheek left no place in the emotions for anything else except for love, and those commandments called for action. Loving God also called for action, the action of always doing that which is right,

45

hereby personifying absolute integrity. Action is reality; rhetoric wishes for reality.

Love, loving all people, transcends political affiliations, religions, or the lack thereof, races, and philosophical concepts. This message of love that Jesus proposes embraces all people. That love includes the basic commandments of Jesus to love God (actionable by doing good) and to love our fellow humans as ourselves (forgiveness, turning the other cheek, etc.). The times that I experience and fully practice this mandate from Jesus have resulted in the absolutely happiest times in my life. It seems like my long search for the ultimate truth has been realized. My mind is still open to any other revelation, however inconceivable.

BELIEVING THAT JESUS IS GOD
TO INHERIT ETERNAL LIFE?

Jesus didn't identify himself as such in the above event with the Pharisee. Many early Christians thought of Jesus as a unique agent of God. The consensus of mainstream Christianity is that for a person to be "saved" means that it is necessary to believe that Jesus is God and that he died for our sins. How can that be? That is not what Jesus told the "teacher of the law." If Jesus is God, is Jesus made in the image of man to the extent that hubris and self-importance define him? Jesus and God rise to a much greater height than this. Doesn't the description of a god obviously made in the image of man negate the concept and image of an omnipotent, loving God? Didn't Jesus teach that we should turn the other cheek, and to forgive our enemies and pray for them, and that the essence of God is love? Having taught that, Jesus would be a liar and a hypocrite if He didn't live by His own commandments.

If there is an original sin, it is selfishness, an instinctive drive of the newly born. We are born with that basic instinct as a way of survival. All young animals, including humans, need to look after their own needs in order to survive. As maturity takes place and survival is solidified, selfishness often remains and is used as a detriment to others. See something you would like to have? Get it, even if you have to kill someone in the process. Selfishness knows no bounds. Helen Keller once wrote a book titled *My Religion*. Her religion was based on the teachings of the theologian and clairvoyant Emanuel Swedenborg, who wrote that God doesn't put anyone into hell. Man puts himself there. And the thing about man that puts him there is his selfishness.

Selfishness is often the precursor of hubris, hostility, and aggression. It is closely associated with Nietzsche's "will to power," which exploits selfishness. Friedrich Nietzsche, a philosopher of the last century, proposed that a "will to power" is the leading motivating force in the human psyche. He also proposed that "God is dead." To the extent that the true nature of God is dead in the minds of people due to the many years of corruptive characterizations of God, that statement has validity.

When asked why he didn't belong to a church, Abraham Lincoln wrote, "When any church will inscribe over its altar, as its sole qualification for membership, the Savior's condensed statement of the substance of both law and Gospel, 'Thou shall love the Lord thy God with all thy heart and with all thy soul and thy neighbor as thyself,' that church will I join with all my heart and all my soul." He rejected the corrupting dogmas of organized religions.

Ted Turner, Lance Armstrong, and Bill Gates have voiced their unbelief in and/or skepticism of God as represented by organized religions. These are men for whom I have great admiration because of their achievements in life. They have promoted charitable works and thus gone around doing a lot of good. They are closer to finding God than they may realize. They are not alone. Many share their beliefs.

It seems that Ted Turner and Lance Armstrong, like so many others, are disenchanted with the God promoted by the organized religions, particularly the mainstream Christians. It is unfortunate that they have limited their view to a God that really does not exist. They may have arrived at the legitimate observation that this view of God, as is commonly held, is suspect. Yet, it is a first step in finding the true God that does exist. The vindictive and vacillating God of fury who wields direct control over every human action does not exist. But what does exist is found in the organized churches and sects that exercise mind control and support slavery of the mind through the process of the guilt trip. Why, even Jim Jones, who started out as a Christian minister doing a lot of good things, ended his ministry by taking nine hundred of his followers to their deaths, even including a physician, a nurse practitioner, and over three hundred innocent children. It is well to observe that anyone who is enriched by the power of control and/or monetary gain for promoting an understanding of God deserves to have his or her legitimacy questioned. God charges no access fee. Jesus Christ, that special messenger of God, revealed the true nature of God. He owned nothing and taught how all mankind could be enriched by following those two commandments that summarized all of the other commandments. An additional truism from Jesus is, "Seek first the kingdom of God and his righteousness, and all these things will be added unto you."

It is well to observe that anyone who is enriched by the power of control and/or monetary gain for promoting an understanding of God deserves to have his or her legitimacy questioned. God accesses no fee. Through the ages, unfortunately, the message from Jesus has been so corrupted and compromised that mainline Christianity can bear little relationship to the spirit of Jesus. Mainsteam religion is so infiltrated with dogmas and misinformation that it can be likened to the inability to see "the forest for the trees." Some of those who have recognized this disparity are as follows:

Bart Ehrman, a leading authority on the Bible and once a strict fundamentalist, now, according to reports, considers himself an agnostic. Much of his work has been concentrated on the early Christian church and how the New Testament Bible was created from many contributing sources. As to its formation and unerring legitimacy, it appears that, as in the spirit of the old English proverb, there's many a slip between the cup and the lip. From his studies, he concludes that the accuracy of the New Testament goes beyond being merely suspect. Forgeries and additions entered into formation of the texts as they changed hands and developed over the course of almost three hundred years. The writings concerning the apocalyptic nature of Jesus can be reasonably attributed to the imagination of Jesus' confused followers.

Yet, the written word or tradition cannot convince or ascertain truth like the experience of a spiritual intervention. Biblical history and analytical studies are no substitute for experiencing that personal relationship with God. This relationship has a spiritual source without reliance on any dubious historical record or tradition accuracy. Sadly, some may not have recognized the opportunity for this spiritual relationship. Does such a relationship require a catastrophic experience or experiences to request this readily available help? The mind's open door invites truth to enter, which in turn allows God to answer.

Anne Rice, a well-known author, has announced that she is leaving Christianity. Once an atheist, and finally finding peace as a Christian, she now contends that mainstream Christianity falls far short of the spirit of Jesus Christ. She tells of finding and experiencing the true meaning of the Christian spirit through Jesus' original teachings (commandments). She comments that faith in Christ is central to her life. She has a lot of company.

Isaac Newton spent as much or more time investigating religion as he did on scientific subjects. He accepted the Arian position that Jesus was created by God and was not the everlasting Son of God, nor did he recognize the concept of the trinity, which the First Council of Nicaea had accepted in 325 AD. For him, Arius prevailed over Athanasius.

Two well-respected independent thinkers and critics of many aspects of the Roman Catholic faith were Desiderius Erasmus and Lord Acton. Erasmus shared the same concerns as Martin Luther, his contemporary. They parted ways when Erasmus decided to remain with the church and attempt changes from within, whereas Luther departed from the church and became very critical of Erasmus' decision not to join him. Lord Acton's actions were very similar to Erasmus', but he was almost excommunicated for his loud vocal criticism of the First Vatican Council in 1868, which decreed papal infallibility.

Albert Schweitzer, the renowned theologian, medical missionary, and organ authority, raised eyebrows with his book *The Quest of the Historical Jesus*. This gave insight into Jesus' life, contrary to the then- and now-current assumptions of the church.

In my opinion, Jimmy Carter appears to be a man of absolute integrity. Here is a Christian, a teacher and deacon in his Baptist church, who upon exiting the presidency of this country, spent his life helping others rather than cashing in on the many lucrative opportunities awaiting ex-presidents. He practiced his Christian beliefs with unselfish action. He is also an example of a person who thinks for himself without being influenced by political agendas of any kind or any source. He left the Southern Baptist Convention, of which he had been a longtime active member, because he saw rigid practices not in line with the legacy of Christ. Here is a man's man, a man who thinks for himself rather than being a captive of others.

These have been loud voices of dissent, yet the organized churches continue to roll on with messages based on misinformation. These messages continue to mislead, either through ignorance or in the interest of power control.

Organized religion complains about losing so many former members with very few new members to take their place. As it turns out, it would be good that the experience of Pogo is recalled: "We have met the enemy, and he is us." If you want to find people who love, join a church. If you want to find people who hate, join a church. That dichotomy exists where selfishness prompts equivocation. Churches are not immune.

THE SECOND CRUCIFIXION OF JESUS

Jesus was crucified as a result of the Jewish leaders accusing Him of heresy and blasphemy. Now, through the corruption of the Christian church, Jesus has been crucified again where Jesus' spirit of love along with His commandments of total love, forgiveness, and turning the other cheek were perceived as inadequate to justify the punishment of heretics. The new Jesus, in the minds of the corrupters, carried a replacement spirit with the message of hate and condemnation of heretics. That same spirit carried on as a natural continuation of the driving force behind the physical crucifixion of Jesus. Through most of the history of Christianity, those who did not believe in the same theology as the church in power were deemed as heretics and suffered the consequences in being tortured and killed by burning at the stake. The inquisitors were in an honored profession in the corrupted Christian church.

Today, the practice of the capital punishment has been replaced, under duress of law. Committing perceived heretics to hell has replaced capital punishment by many seminaries, Bible schools, and churches. Many Bible colleges teach about the Bible, but the spirit of Jesus can be lost when these colleges brainwash their students by promoting the proposition that as graduates, they become the ultimate authority on the true relationship with God. They are empowered with the authority to condemn others to hell for a perceived blasphemy and heresy. This exclusive group might well be known as the "Burning at the Stake Society," or "Give 'em Hell Society." Hasn't the spirit of Jesus been replaced by the Nietzsche's "will to power" and hubris? All of this is easily traceable to the selfishness property of the human ego with its resulting arrogance. No one outside the fundamentalist churches escapes this condemnation. Yet these practitioners of condemnation and intolerance seem to be oblivious to the very Bible verses they would protect, such as from Jesus,

"Judge not, lest you be judged in the same manner in which you judge others." Tradition tends to conveniently blind the eyes of the Holier Than Thou club.

Tradition also appears to play a leading role in the practice of condemning heretics and their punishment. It seems to have originated with those Roman emperors, including Nero, who condemned and killed those who refused to recognize the emperor as a god. Many early Christians suffered and were killed under those circumstances. Later on, the Orthodox Christian church was recognized as the official religion of the Roman Empire. As Lord Acton once stated, "Power tends to corrupt, and absolute power corrupts absolutely." Those in control of the church adopted the tradition of the earlier Roman emperors: death to heretics, usually accompanied by torture, such as by being burned to death at the stake. Just where was the spirit of Jesus? It was washed away by the hubris of man. That same tradition continues to this day, though mortal punishment has been eliminated where law has interfered. The teachings of churches and Bible schools based on tradition are highly suspect because of their dogmas that deviate from Jesus' commandments and His spirit of love.

In spite of the above observations about organized religion, many of these churches are to be commended for the good that results from their existence. Good deeds and good works are often felt in the communities they serve. Families are brought together. They are also the source of many people congregating together. Members find support and friendship as they worship and serve side by side.

A PRESCRIPTION FOR A HAPPY LIFE

My having received the gift of a new life has proven to me that the prescription for a lasting happy life is one that is easy to fill: Love God through the action of doing that which is good, and always personify integrity. Love all people through the action of doing unto others as you would have them do unto you, with hostility toward none. This manifests itself by turning the other cheek and by not easily taking offense: forgive all enemies and pray for them. Encourage people and you will be encouraged! Eliminate selfishness from life. Vanquish anger and hostility. Take care of your body by strengthening it through exercise. Be prepared for the downside of exercise, which can increase the production of testosterone. Testosterone, in turn, promotes aggression and hostility. Never do anything that would harm the body. Have reverence for all life. Enjoy and become alive with nature. Make uplifting music a part of life; sing often; interact in a positive manner with many people, enjoying their presence. As previously noted, living without the presence of people as a matrix and conduit in life is the same as being in a swimming pool without water. Keep an open mind, so that it would be receptive to truth as it reveals itself. Be receptive to the experience of a spiritual entity that does exist, in order to receive personal security and serenity. Acknowledge the true God that does exist and don't be misled by a faith and tradition that history, logic, and experience have proven to be a fallacy. This is more than a wish list; it's a To Do list for today, tomorrow, and the rest of our lives on this earth.

Anyone who truly desires to live a happy life has that opportunity by following the above prescription to the letter. The only prerequisite is an absolute dedication to that end. It's one day at a time with the reward of happiness, total peace of mind, and freedom, with the anticipation of the life after death, which is the extension of the ladder we begin to climb while we are still alive.

Now, wait a moment. Is personal happiness the most desirable purpose of life? Well, yes, all other objectives are means toward that end. Yet, for this discussion, it is the ultimate happiness that represents the pinnacle of the human desire. A suicide bomber is happy for his/her purpose until his/her own hand extinguishes the perpetrator's life. People who do evil acts and exercise evil control over others are happy for their momentary "will to power" successes. It appears that the etiology of any evil act is selfishness. Those who seek happiness for selfish reasons find themselves chasing an illusion. Such happiness is built on the accumulation of happy events. Eventually, the happiness evolved from this source finds itself crushed under its own weight. That has been my experience, and to my dismay, having followed the above philosophy, based on selfishness, for so many years. Now, with this revelation of the ultimate everlasting happy life prescription, built on positive, uplifting, unselfish motives with the love for all people, the spirit of God's love saturates my very being. Am I the happiest person in the world? From where I stand, I could be. I can't answer for others, yet having known so many kind, unselfish, positive and gracious people who project a contagious euphoria, I must have a lot of company. The consequence for everyone following the above prescription would be a world without war, a world without crime, a world of peace, a world where the lost war on drugs would be solved.

Again, to point at the culprit, hubris, radiating from the "will to power," seems to be at the center of the corruption of all that is good, whether it be religion, government, or family values. Resisting this evil wave through violence becomes a celebration and support of hubris itself and is thus self-defeating, as is fighting war with war. A landmark book on war and its etiology can be found in *All Quiet on the Western Front* by a World War I German soldier. This is a reading that should be mandated in all of our schools. Our political leaders should be knowledgeable about this philosophy, rather than sink under the influence from Machiavelli's *The Prince*, a book that is said to have been by the bedside of both Adolf Hitler and Joseph Stalin. Is war a glorious undertaking? Time Life's DVD *Apocalypse WWII* illustrates the very horror of militaristic conflict.

Does the concept of turning the other cheek have limitations? Should we resist the probability of dying while being attacked by another? A basic human instinct is to live, to survive. We have each been given a life to live, as has the attacker. In this instance, if only one were to survive this encounter, the innocent should prevail over the aggressor. Where certain death is not imminent, consider the actions of passive resistance as followed by Mohandas Gandhi and Martin Luther King Jr. in their victorious campaigns.

It has been reported that in one of Gandhi's passive resistance demonstrations, the police were beating demonstrators in order to get them to move. One woman, after having been beaten to the ground, found the club dropped by her attacker. She reached over, picked it up, and handed it to her attacker with the words, "Excuse me, sir, you dropped this." This act represented passive resistance in the spirit of Christ.

As to war among nations or other adversaries, is there any justification for killing a perceived enemy? There has been much written about "just wars." The countries of the west often quote Augustine of Hippo's views on this subject. A close analysis reveals justification is often gained through a great distortion of Augustine's basic premise on the subject. The spirit of Christianity then gives way to narcissistic hubris.

Is not the one and true religion where Jesus indicated, "The Kingdom of God is within you" and "Love God with all of your heart, all of your mind and all of your strength, and love your neighbor as yourself"? This, with its ramifications, encompasses all religions that propose the same theology. Exit the hubristic nature and selfishness of man and enter truth. Unfortunately, the message of Christ, leading to Christianity, has been corrupted right from the moment of His death by many surviving disciples/apostles and inaccurate interpretations and recordings of their works. This corruption continues to the present day.

As I was on the path to death, trying with all my might to enter that portal, the door to life was eventually revealed. Having been denied entry through the door to death, I found the door to knowledge and truth opened. All of my previous thoughts about "faith alone" invited complacency. But the way to a full life and the path to heaven is uncomplicated: simply loving all people and loving God, through the system described by Jesus. It is that and that alone. God does exist, and divine intervention confirmed the presence of a special messenger from God, Jesus. The true Jesus with His spirit is limited to His expressed words found in the Gospels. The distinct impression from my death's door experience is that I survived in order to publicize the message revealed to me.

Failure to conceptualize and fully practice this love for all people can have fatal consequences for type A personalities. How can that be? Type As often carry hostility and negative emotions in personal relationships or directed as concepts in their persona, leading to high stress levels. This results in the rise of cortisol levels, which tends to clog up arteries and lead to myocardial infarcts. Most programs aimed at reducing heart attack risks attempt to address this problem of hostility, along with requiring special heart diets. The programs are often not very successful in altering lifestyles and attitudes involving hostility. A positive modification of personality traits is much more difficult to achieve, yet offers the best results. Jesus commanded that we love everyone, forgive and pray for those who persecute us, and turn the other cheek. As a type A personality with its ingrained and innate hostility characteristic, I found that the most challenging project of my life was to develop the constant habit of "turning the other cheek." After many failures, success was finally mine. It took a long time and hard work, but the results have been astounding. Goodbye to stress and to its consequences. Every time I drive my car, I welcome the challenges experienced with hostile drivers. The tranquil mind means a tranquil body and with it, a healthy body. Prior to initiating the program to love all people (phase two), whereby all hostility vanished, I had been on a very strict no-fat, low-sugar, vegetarian diet for many years (phase one). Yet, in that period of time (phase one), I've had numerous heart attacks and many coronary stents implanted to open coronary arteries. Since entering phase two in May 2009, my cardiovascular system seems to be in the best condition it has seen in more than twenty years. Witness my snow shoveling experience in January of 2010. During this time, there has never been a scintilla of a hint concerning cardiovascular compromise. Yet, during this latter time, because of feeling so good and as a way of celebration, I've been known to pig out on the fatty foods and sugary deserts I had previously avoided for so long. Admittedly, this was not a good idea. The absence of hostility in my psyche has been the defining element in reversing the trend of advancing heart disease (fortified by an inherited trait) in my body. The pursuit and complete practice of loving all people through the mechanics enumerated by Jesus has become the magic bullet. Are you listening, Dick Cheney? We both have had parallel history of heart disease.

HOW CHOCOLATE COOKIES CURED MY HEART DISEASE

In the fall of 2010, I had been feeling so good; there was absolutely the need to celebrate. For a period of at least six months, the celebration had taken the form of eating all of the junk food that I had avoided during the previous sixteen years. Ah, chocolate cookies had met their master. I easily ate through a bag of eight large cookies at one sitting. They were so good. There were other foods that were sweet with fat that I began to enjoy after their absence of sixteen years.

Yet, there appeared to be uncertainty on my part as to the potential for that diet to cause harm to my body and especially to my heart. This concern resulted in a call to my cardiologist, Dr. Hantman, requesting an exercise stress test. He convinced me that it should be an echocardiogram stress test.

Several weeks later, Dr. Freidman was ready to check my endurance. I requested that he not stop the exercise treadmill until I yelled, "Uncle." Dr. Friedman was very flexible and cooperative. During the exercise, as it progressed, he advised that if I reached the next stage, I would have gone further than anyone else over eighty years of age during his eight years of giving that test. I reached the next stage with a little to spare. With that, in answer to my question, Dr Friedman said that I could shovel all of the snow I wanted to shovel.

Needless to say, on subsequently reviewing the results, Dr. Hantman was greatly pleased with the results. I had reached a high level in the exercise test without ischemia and also reached my maximum heart rate. That was my best result from a stress test in almost sixteen years. Previously, ischemia was always present and maximum heart rate unattainable. During the previous sixteen years, as mentioned before, I had experienced five heart attacks, had a quadruple coronary bypass surgery, and required nine coronary stent insertions. I had also eaten all of the right foods while avoiding the junk food. Now, my heart wasn't getting worse with age, it was getting better, and heart disease was reversing its trend, junk food to the contrary.

Chocolate chip cookies to the rescue! Well, not exactly. It does not take a genius to conclude that the stress test turned out so well in spite of the junk food, not because of it. The defining difference was found in the change in my lifestyle, where the mind was dictating a healthy body and heart. That change came about when I was led to fully follow Jesus' commandments to love God (all that is just and good) and to love all people without qualification. This concept included forgiveness and the ability to "turn the other cheek."

Jesus' commandments were not meant as mere rhetoric but as a mandate to be followed completely and at all times. Those commandments became a permanent part of my psyche as a result of the "door to death experience." I had always liked the words and found merit in those words, yet I only attempted to follow them when it suited my fancy and didn't interfere with my selfish nature. Yes, I was free at last of any hostility, hate, resentment, and other negative emotions. And free of heart disease, as a consequence. The disadvantage of the type A personality had been overcome.

DISCOVERING THE MEANING OF LIFE

What is the meaning of life? Seek the truth with an open mind and accept truth as it is revealed. Without an open mind, a person is stuck in a quagmire of his or her own making. Regardless of a person's religious affiliation, the pathway to finding and experiencing God is through positive interaction with mankind, more particularly in the scenario as described by Jesus' answer to the teacher of the law. Any other additional faith based belief, such as that found in organized religions, doesn't distract from or add to that basic pathway to God, even if one were to believe that the earth is flat or the sun revolves around the earth. Yet, any religion that advocates killing people, more particularly innocent people, falls fatally short of legitimacy and exhibits the flaws of hubris and an ingrained selfishness through the "will to power." Be wary of those who allow hate and malice to penetrate their agenda, especially when done so in the name of Christianity or any other religion. The spirit of Christ is only present in an agenda filled with love. Are the names of Jesus and God synonymous with love or hate? The agenda with malice exposes the hubristic evil in the promoter of hate and malice. The way to experiencing God is through construction and not destruction. Construction builds the relationship; destruction tears down and destroys that relationship.

I've experienced pure joy when opportunities allow me to uplift others. Yet, in spite of my best intentions, words from me can unintentionally have the opposite effect. To celebrate our long-standing friendships, several of my friends and I had a reunion on our seventieth birthday. In the normal course of conversation, we asked each other, "How are you doing? How are you feeling?" At that age, some of us had experienced some physical setbacks.

When asked how I was doing, I responded, "I'm feeling great, never felt better in my life! I'd rather be my age now than any age before now."

Much later, one of my friends told me that there was one present who confided to him, "The more he talked, the worse I felt." From that conversation, I learned that a truthful answer to an innocent question might have negative consequences. I vowed that from then on, whenever the question was asked about my wellbeing, my answer would be modified in consideration for the other person's comparative health infirmities.

Ah yes, how easy it is to forget. Just recently, I called a friend to inquire about his health status, since he had just returned from a hospital stay. After hearing about his recent experience, he asked, "So how are you doing?"

My immediate response: "Great, if not better."

He replied, "Well, good for you." I knew right then that I had just made the mistake which I had vowed not to make. Never again!

FINAL THOUGHTS

I find no mystery as to why so many people are leaving churches and why so many have gravitated to agnosticism and atheism. Christian churches and others have stubbornly held to ancient beliefs and traditions that oppose well-founded scientific evidence. The Catholic Church finally acknowledges that the earth revolves around the sun. This acknowledgement didn't take place until several hundred years after the death of the persecuted Galileo. Yet many inconsistencies remain, especially within the field of evolution. Then there are the traditional teachings of the mainline Christian churches that describe God as egocentric, vindictive, capable of fury, etc., all of which are foibles characteristic of mankind. Is God so egocentric that those who don't believe in that entity will be punished, put into hell? If so, this God is made in the image of the Roman emperor Nero, who condemned people to death for not believing that he was a god. Thus, as described by tradition, the writers of this position effectively have made the concept of God in the image of man with all of man's weaknesses to be unbelievable to minds of independent thought. If many of the church's positions can't be sustained, how can any part of it have authenticity? These are reasonable questions and conclusions.

Then, there is the all-too-obvious religious hypocrisy. The Christian religion is based on the teachings of Jesus Christ, who represented love for everyone and presented God as a loving God. Yet, all of these representations have been compromised by the actions of "Christians" throughout history as an antithesis to the truth that Christ, by his own words, came to reveal: love for God, with its implications, and love for all mankind. Hate and malice were not a part of Jesus' vocabulary of positive action. Unfortunately, the noise of the hypocrisy drowns out the beautiful music of the messenger.

Jesus' simple commandments will reveal the ultimate truth as to a fulfilled life and the destiny of mankind. We were born to enjoy life, not to be enslaved by our own selfishness or a guilt complex. Jesus' simple commandments were to love God through the action of integrity and to love people through the actions of turning the other cheek, forgiving others, and praying for their wellbeing, all in the process of building all people up. Jesus announced that those who followed His commandments would know the truth and the truth would set them free. This is the opportunity to exercise the scientific method by following these commandments to experience the results for the purpose of exposure or validation. Having put this to the test, my experience completely validates Jesus' position. For me, it has resulted in a wonderful, euphoric experience, freedom from being controlled, the most self-confidence in my life, and greatly improved health. Along with this, I experience the spiritual presence of Jesus in my life. Does the ultimate authority for my life and my activity come from the Bible or any man's would-be control? No, it comes from my communion with the spirit of God, through Jesus, who is constantly with me. There is no person and no book to exercise control over me; I am free. The spirit of God through Jesus is my strength.

How can it be that a person can experience the spirit of God in his/her life? There is no scientific experiment that can prove it. Yet, there are personal experiences that exist but may not be provable by the scientific method. As an example, when I was nine years old and sick in bed in my home, I heard the sound of my father's truck coming down the driveway on the opposite side of the house from my bedroom. At that moment, without being able to see the truck and with no foreknowledge, though a vision in my mind's eye, I was surprised to see a blue bicycle in the bed of the pickup truck as it advanced down the driveway. I heard the truck engine stop and my father opening the kitchen door. I couldn't see him, but I heard him holler, "Frederick, do you feel well enough to come out here for a minute?" Wow, I knew I needed to act surprised. How was I to otherwise know what was out there for me? And there it was, in the back of the truck, the very same bicycle I had seen it in my mind's eye. Previously, there had been some talk of my getting a bicycle for Christmas when I would be twelve years old. Yet, that talk hadn't occurred in the recent months. As it turned out, my father, an electrical contractor who worked alone, frequently would go on a job and return at night. If the job were close to home, he would come home for lunch. This day, when he left the house, he had anticipated going to a short-lasting job and then proceeding to Kemp's Department Store and there buying himself a suit. At the last minute, before proceeding to Kemp's, he decided to buy me a bicycle instead of his suit. He had not anticipated that action beforehand and my mother knew nothing about it. It turned out to be a spontaneous act.

This was the only experience like this in my life. It happened, yet its occurrence cannot be scientifically proven. Others may have had similar experiences. I have previously written about how the spirit of God's presence has guided and protected me throughout the many catastrophic events of my life.

I have shown how arrogance and closed minds have corrupted the Christian religion. The same can be said of the closed minds in the scientific community. The existence of God is impossible, according to scientific reasoning? According to many in the scientific community, there are proven impossible concepts, such as that of the perpetual motion device and man's ability to produce absolute zero. At one time, according to the then-curent knowledge of aerodynamics, the bumblebee shouldn't be able to fly. However the bumblebee didn't know of that scientific impossibility. At one time, the scientific method couldn't support the concept of space travel or man's flight through air. Closed minds adamantly shut off the possibilities. Yet eventually, as water seeks its own level, so too will science and religion meld into the ultimate truth and stand on equal ground.

Sir Isaac Newton, James Maxwell, and Albert Einstein are generally recognized as the three greatest minds in the history of science. At least two of these believed in the existence of God and a personal God. Albert Einstein is not necessarily the exception, only to the extent that he may not have believed in a personal God. The great mathematician Blaise Pascal embraced the concept of a personal God after a life-threatening experience. The list goes on and on.

Now comes the test of probability as to my personal experience with conceivable miracles.

1. What is the probability of an eighty-three-year-old man surviving

a massive hemorrhagic stroke of the magnitude described by the radiologist's CT scan report?

2.   What is the probability of this same man, with a history of heart damage from four previous coronary infarcts and lung damage from a previous severe pneumonia episode, surviving a heart attack and double pneumonia complications of this hemorrhagic stroke? Consider that this man wanted to die and tried to die as this chain of mortal dimensions compromised his stroke recovery.

3.   What is the probability that this man would recover without any evidence of ever having had a stroke? This revealed the absence of the expected and presumably consequential hydrocephalic outcome.

4.   What is the probability that this same eighty-three-year-old man's recovery would result in a vast improvement in his mental and physical capacity over that prior to his stroke with its complications?

My experience with the door to death is just as unprovable as my experience with the blue bicycle of my youth. Proof is not necessary for a personal experience of this kind. Proof is in the experience that remains unchallenged by other explanations. Were these miracles due to divine intervention? I leave this to those with open and unbiased minds to decide.

The incident of my physical recovery was accompanied by the revelation of the meaning of life itself. This revelation couldn't have come from a vacuum. It would have to be from what can only be identified as God. My continued faith in the spirit of God through Jesus being constantly with me through all of my catastrophic experiences was reinforced by the revelation. It became the answer to my lifelong quest in seeking truth, wherever it would take me.

Revealed: there is a God, a God never adequately explained by the writings of man. God is not an egocentric, malicious, and vindictive God. An egocentric God, as in the image of Emperor Nero, would insist that the unbeliever be tossed into hell as an unbeliever. That concept excites the militaristic nature of many mainstream religions. The true God exceeds all of the limitations in the man-likeness God as written about in the Bible and possibly elsewhere. God is the spirit that defies adequate explanation due to the limited experience of man and the boundaries of our mind. Yet we can know that nature is given its own laws upon which to operate, as if the ability of nature to do so has been a delegated authority. God does have at least one spiritual messenger where divine providence can manifest itself through personal intervention as by particular providence. My experience has shown that the spiritual messenger for me has been Jesus. This spirit has never identified itself as Jesus, but fits in perfectly with Jesus' basic teachings.

This revelation supports the words of Jesus. Jesus, by His own words, tells us that He was born to reveal the truth. The truth is that God represents love and all that is positive. Negativity does not exist in God. Jesus' truth is revealed in His commandments to love everyone. This is fortified by the instruction of forgiveness and turning the other cheek.

The message that was so loudly proclaimed to me was that the pathway to finding God and the meaning of life is through positive interaction with people. Loving all people is the beginning of the process and an integral component in a beautiful and fulfilled life. Experiencing this phenomenon leads us to experiencing God, an entity of love, justice, and creative ability. People on earth were born for the purpose of enjoying life. We have been provided with the passageway toward that end. This has been my experience as my life has been renewed. It does take work to arrive at this perfect harmony. The work involves eliminating selfishness from our lives. It involves consistently turning the other cheek and the absolute love for all people with the practice of forgiveness.

This required work is in opposition to the human nature of egocentricity. It can be difficult to overcome our innate trait of selfishness. Yet, it is only through this process that we can truly appreciate life and optimally experience the spirit of God. Bad habits can be difficult to break. Good habits can be difficult to make. Both efforts challenge our resolve. Establishing the habit of automatic love and all that it encompasses is not easy, but the most worthwhile of any habit. Proof is shown to those who would enter this process.

CHRISTIAN PRINCIPLES IN PRACTICE

To forgive is to experience the joy of a Christian life. How does that apply to an event where an assailant maliciously murders a loved one? Here, is it necessary or even possible to forgive? Yet, there are news reports of people who have forgiven those who have fostered this ultimate criminal act against a loved one. There are even instances where this act of forgiving also led to assimilating the assailant into the family of the aggrieved. In the criminal justice system, there are also those innocents who have served long terms in jail, often due to prosecutorial misconduct. Many of these victims have expressed an absence of resentment for the unjustified confinement but gratification for the final outcome. Forgiveness is the basis for their response, often based on their religious beliefs that required forgiveness.

Is this taking the concept of forgiving too far? It is to the naturally vindictive mind. Such an act of violence or injustice is only satisfied by anger, or is it? That anger is never satisfied, even with the enactment of the ultimate penalty provided by the legal system. This anger is only extinguished with the death of the aggrieved or the aggrieved's ability to forgive. On the other hand, consider the person or persons who have not only forgiven the murderer of their child or a loved one, but have made a friend of that person. Is the forgiver some sort of nut or what? That appears to be the normal, emotional gut feeling of the average human psyche. Yet, beyond the knee-jerk reaction to that act of forgiveness, what are the results? The mind of the forgiver is no longer under the control of the trespasser. The forgiver has initiated the response of a forgiveness that not only is self-satisfying but in turn has also led to positive advances in the life of the perpetrator. What a victory for humanity! The forgiver has overcome the natural human emotion of vindictiveness, which resulted in the positive emotional experience. Peace of mind, is there any substitute?

This illustrates the practical results of following the teachings of Jesus: love your enemies, forgive them, and pray for those who persecute you. Love people; love all people, including the unlovable. All of these teachings seem contrary to human nature. The words are not mere rhetoric. It is a call to a higher status. Reaching that higher status elevates us in our ability to experience God in our lives.

As the result of the divine intervention that saved my life by bringing me back from death's door, I received not only a renewed body but also a special revelation as to that which is the true God, a God of all people. In addition, a path to a happy life follows as the love for all people develops. The pathway to finding God is filled with people, the absolute love for all people. With that, God can and will be experienced. It is as simple and as difficult as following the commandments of Jesus: love everyone, forgive anyone who has done you or a loved one harm, turn the other cheek, and thus not be offended. Jesus rightly predicts that those who follow this procedure will know the truth and the truth will set them free. This pathway is filled with a happy life and is continued beyond the door of death. Everyone entering the state of death carries their thoughts from life into that next entity. Thus, a person with all good, kind, and loving thoughts is placed in what many describe as heaven, whereas those with malicious, hostile, and evil thoughts proceed into the state of hell. Everyone determines their destiny after death by their own actions and thought patterns in life while traveling along on that continuous pathway. The lone belief that there is a God, that Jesus is God, or any other representation of this nature, is not enough by itself to alter that pathway. Those who feel otherwise will discover the truth as the door to their life on earth is closed and the path that they traveled in life continues.

The body and the soul are energized through positive interaction with people. The love for all people and the appreciation for the wonderful gift of nature lead us to recognize that there is a true, loving God. God can and does provide a particular providence through a special messenger or messengers. As we mature in loving all people, without qualification, insight produces the fertile field where unimaginable happiness and peace of mind grow exponentially. The knowledge of God then blossoms forth as a natural consequence of our experience.

The familiarity of enjoying the knowledge and advantages of the spiritual presence of a true God is open to those who would approach this adventure with an open mind. Closed minds shut the door to truth. No religion owns an exclusive relationship with God. Hubris may deny that statement. Man may play favorites, but God, as the Supreme Being, embraces all. The ability to find and experience God is open to all who seek that divine nature.

God's presence is exposed to every individual through the process of love. That love starts with loving people, all people, which leads to loving God. The indwelling spirit of God is an experience that proves God's existence and is proportional to the love we have demonstrated in our actions and thoughts toward other people. Everyone who passes though the door of death will find the truth revealed as a revelation from God. The entrance through that door was denied me, but God revealed to me that truth which I had long sought after. I can choose to love, and I can choose to hate. As to people, I choose to love. The result speaks for itself. This writing expresses the essence of God's answer.

There is great beauty in the life that goes beyond merely existing. A full life utilizes the spiritual nature of man. The spiritual nature of man is fulfilled through experiencing God in our lives as our love for all mankind is matured. That flame of love incinerates all hostilities and malice. We can deny it, but we cannot extinguish its flame.